BUFFALO BILL

LEGENDS OF THE WEST

BUFFALO BILL

Published by Creative Education, 123 South Broad Street, Mankato, Minnesota 56001
Creative Education is an imprint of The Creative Company
Design and Production by EvansDay Design

Photographs by Buffalo Bill Historical Center; Cody, Wyoming (*P.69.137*, cover, p. 2; *P.69.1790*, p.35; *P.69.118*, p. 38; *P.69.121*, p. 45), Corbis (Bettmann, Hulton—Deutsch Collection, Lake County Museum, John McAnulty, Medford Historical Society Collection, Kevin R. Morris, David Muench, Owaki—Kulla, ML Sinibaldi, Paul A. Souders, Swim Ink), The Granger Collection, New York

Library of Congress Cataloging-in-Publication Data
Goodman, Michael E. Buffalo Bill / by Michael E. Goodman.
p. cm. — (Legends of the West)
Includes index.
ISBN 1-58341-336-7

1. Buffalo Bill, 1846-1917—Juvenile literature. 2. Pioneers—West (U.S.)—Biography—Juvenile literature. 3. Frontier and pioneer life—West (U.S.)—Juvenile literature. 4. Entertainers—United States—Biography—Juvenile literature. 5. Buffalo Bill's Wild West Show—Juvenile literature. 6. West (U.S.)—Biography—Juvenile literature. I. Title. II. Legends of the West (Mankato, Minn.)
F594.B94G66 2005   978.02'092—dc22   2004058231 [B]

First edition

2 4 6 8 9 7 5 3 1

Cover and page 2 photograph:
Will "Buffalo Bill" Cody as a young man, displaying his famous facial hair

Michael E. Goodman

ON JANUARY 11, 1917,
MUCH OF EUROPE WAS AT WAR, AND THE UNITED STATES WAS PREPARING TO JOIN IN, TOO.

But for that one day, **World War I** took a back seat in global newspapers to a bigger story—the announcement that Buffalo Bill Cody had died the day before at his sister May's house in Denver, Colorado.

Telegrams poured in from

government leaders in the U.S. and around the world. Even such enemies as the king of England and the kaiser of Germany joined in mourning Buffalo Bill's death.

Buffalo Bill would have loved the attention. He always enjoyed being in the spotlight. Early in his life, Will Cody was a Western pioneer, delivering mail for the Pony Express, fighting in the Civil War, killing buffalo to feed the men building the transcontinental railroad, and scouting in the Indian wars. Then, he spent more than 45 years as a show business pioneer, bringing the Wild West to life for audiences around the world. His real-life adventures were almost as exciting as those portrayed on the stage or described in hundreds of dime novels. No one knew—or cared—just where truth stopped and legend began.

CHAPTER ONE

Riding into History

The wild, exciting life of

WILLIAM FREDERICK "BUFFALO BILL" CODY

STARTED TRAGICALLY.

Will was born near LeClaire, Iowa,

ON FEBRUARY 26, 1846—

the fourth child and second son

of Isaac and Mary Ann Cody. When Will was six years old,

he watched as his older brother, Samuel, was thrown from

a horse and crushed to death. Will's mother took the death

so badly that Isaac soon decided to move the family to a

farm in the Salt Creek valley near Leavenworth, Kansas.

At the time, Kansas was a new territory whose residents were divided on whether slavery should be allowed there. Kansans didn't just argue about slavery; they had violent confrontations over the issue. Isaac's neighbors insisted on knowing where he stood. At first, he tried to avoid voicing his opinion but finally was coerced into speaking out. As Isaac stood at a podium and announced that he was opposed to slavery spreading into Kansas, a man jumped out of the crowd and knifed him in the back, puncturing a lung. Isaac survived the knifing but never fully recovered. Three years later, he died, forcing 11-year-old Will to quit school and look for a job to support the family.

Will was hired by the Russell, Majors, and Waddell Company, which handled freight and mail service between Kansas and areas farther west. He served as a messenger on wagon trains and as a teamster, caring for the teams of oxen and mules that pulled the company's huge Conestoga wagons.

During one of his first wagon train trips, Will helped fend off an Indian attack. As he was preparing to settle in for the night, Will spotted the silhouette of a warrior in front of him. The Indian was aiming an arrow at another teamster. Will quickly brought his rifle to his shoulder and fired. Soon after, people in Leavenworth started calling Will "the youngest Indian slayer of the plains."

In 1860, the Russell, Majors, and Waddell Company embarked on an exciting new business venture—the Pony Express. At the time, the U.S. government was looking for an efficient way to get mail to the many Americans who had moved to California

Young Will Cody found work as a wagon train messenger and teamster. On one of his first trips, he helped repel an Indian attack.

PONY EXPRESS!

CHANGE OF

TIME !

REDUCED

RATES !

10 Days to San Francisco!

LETTERS

WILL BE RECEIVED AT THE

OFFICE, 84 BROADWAY,

NEW YORK,

Up to **4** P. M. every TUESDAY,

AND

Up to **2½** P. M. every SATURDAY,

Which will be forwarded to connect with the PONY EXPRESS leaving
ST. JOSEPH, Missouri,

Every WEDNESDAY and SATURDAY at 11 P. M.

TELEGRAMS

Sent to Fort Kearney on the mornings of MONDAY and FRIDAY, will connect with **PONY** leaving St. Joseph, WEDNESDAYS and SATURDAYS.

The Pony Express operated only for some 18 months, but it added an adventurous and memorable chapter to America's Wild West.

following the 1849 gold rush. Since the transcontinental railroad had not yet been completed, a relay system of horseback riders carrying mail pouches seemed like the best idea. A series of stations would be set up 10 to 15 miles (16—24 km) apart on the 1,800-mile (2,900 km) stretch between St. Joseph, Missouri, and Sacramento, California. Each rider would travel approximately 75 miles (120 km) as quickly as possible, switching to fresh horses at each station, and then hand off the mail pouch to the next rider. It seemed pretty simple—if one didn't factor in bad weather, rough terrain, horses tripping in prairie dog holes, and attacks by bandits or hostile bands of Indians.

Russell, Majors, and Waddell signed a contract with the government to establish the system and then put the following advertisement in newspapers:

WANTED

young, skinny, wiry fellows, not over 18. Must
be expert riders, willing to risk death daily.
Orphans preferred. Wages $25 a week.

To skinny, 14-year-old Will Cody, the chance to find adventure and make $25 a week (comparable to around $550/week today) sounded great. He applied and was hired as the youngest rider in the Pony Express.

The Pony Express thrilled most Americans and won a warm place in U.S. history, but it was a business failure. After operating the system for only 18 months—from April 1860 until November

Wild Bill Hickok

James Butler Hickok lived a short but illustrious life as one of the Wild West's most accomplished gunfighters. Born in 1837 in Illinois, he left home for Kansas in 1855. In 1860, Hickok joined the Pony Express, where he became friends with Will Cody. The next year, he shot and killed three men in a dispute over money but was released after successfully arguing that the killings were done in self-defense. The incident earned him the nickname "Wild Bill." Hickok later served as a Union Army scout under General George Armstrong Custer, who noted that his "skill in the use of a rifle and pistol was unerring." He served briefly as sheriff of both Hays City and Abilene, Kansas, but spent most of his time gambling. Hickok was involved in a number of gunfights and became the subject of many newspaper articles and dime novels. He spent two seasons touring with *Buffalo Bill's Wild West* but decided that acting was not for him. In 1876, he followed the gold rush to Deadwood, South Dakota, where he was murdered while playing poker.

1861—Russell, Majors, and Waddell went bankrupt. Will was out of a job, but he did have some money to bring home to his family, and he had made a good friend in fellow rider James "Wild Bill" Hickok.

The Civil War was already underway when the Pony Express died out, and Will was eager to join the Union Army. His mother was very ill, however, and he promised her he would stay home for a while. When Mary Ann died in December 1863, Will joined up with the Seventh Kansas Cavalry, serving as a teamster, messenger, and occasional scout. His most exciting duty involved going undercover as a spy in Tennessee. Will put on a Southern accent and spent time behind Confederate lines trying to learn what the enemy forces were planning. It was his first job as an actor.

Early in 1865, 19-year-old Will was assigned to work as an orderly at a Union Army hospital in St. Louis, Missouri. There he met a beautiful 22-year-old woman named Louisa Frederici, and the two fell in love. She described the slim, six-foot-tall (1.8 m) soldier as being "handsome, clean-shaven . . . graceful, lithe, smooth in his movements and the modulations of his speech . . . quite the most wonderful man I had ever known." They courted briefly and married on March 6, 1866. Then they moved from St. Louis back to Leavenworth, where Will promised to settle down. From the start, the couple seemed mismatched. Louisa was reserved, while Will was outgoing. She dressed simply and conservatively, and he loved fancy clothes. She wanted a quiet home life, and he was eager for adventure.

For a brief time, Will attempted to turn the boardinghouse his mother had run in Leavenworth into a hotel, but he had little business skill. What he did best was to entertain hotel guests with stories of his adventures on the trail and in the army. He quickly decided that the stay-at-home life was really not for him; he needed more excitement. Will found work as a stagecoach driver and then joined Wild Bill Hickok as a scout for the U.S. Cavalry. He moved Louisa and their new daughter, Arta, to western Kansas, closer to where he worked, though Louisa was not thrilled to be living on the frontier. Will let his hair grow long in the style of Western scouts, grew a mustache and goatee, and clothed himself in a buckskin outfit that Louisa had sewn for him.

Will was an outstanding tracker and loved spending his days on horseback. When he heard that the Kansas Pacific Railroad was hiring men to hunt buffalo to feed the workers laying track across the plains, he jumped at the chance. He didn't realize it at the time, but taking the hunting job would help turn Will from an adventurer into a legend.

Yellow Hand's Hair

Many different legends developed from the battle at War Bonnet Creek in which Buffalo Bill killed and scalped the Cheyenne leader Yellow Hand, whose name is sometimes translated "Yellow Hair." As the stories were repeated, they grew and grew. No other soldier ever reported that Will shouted, "The first scalp for Custer!" though he may have done so. More likely, Will invented the quote to show his strong feelings about the death of Custer and his men. Another legend tells how Will decided, after the fight, to send his wife, Louisa, a package containing Yellow Hand's scalp and feathered headdress. He sent her a message to tell her to expect an unusual present. Unfortunately, the package arrived before the message. Louisa opened the box, saw the bloody scalp inside, and fainted. While Louisa often repeated this story, she later admitted that it was not true. Will kept the scalp and headdress with his belongings and later displayed them at *Wild West* performances.

CHAPTER TWO

Western Hero, Eastern Actor

WILL CODY QUICKLY EARNED A REPUTATION AS THE
FINEST BUFFALO HUNTER
ON THE PLAINS. ACCORDING TO FELLOW HUNTER
Bat Masterson—who would later
BECOME A WESTERN LEGEND HIMSELF—
Cody had an unmatchable style.

He would "ride his horse full tilt into a herd of buffalo, and, with a pistol in either hand and the bridle reins between his teeth, was almost sure to bring down the day's supply of meat at the first run. With six shots in each pistol, he often killed as many as eight buffalos on a run."

"Buffalo Bill" Cody cut a striking image, which would help attract West enthusiasts in his show business days to come.

One time, Will and another hunter named Bill Comstock competed to see who could bring down the most animals in an eight-hour period. The winner would earn the nickname "Buffalo Bill." The contest wasn't even close. Cody killed 69 buffalo that day, compared to his opponent's 46, and the title was his. Will spent eight months as the king of the buffalo hunters. He claimed to have killed 4,280 buffalo to feed hungry railroad workers.

While Buffalo Bill gained fame from buffalo hunting, today the killing of the buffalo remains a sad chapter in American history. Between 1850 and 1890, hunters slaughtered nearly 20 million buffalo, until they were almost extinct. Unlike Will, many greedy hunters killed the animals simply for their skins, leaving the meat to rot wastefully on the ground. Since Native Americans on the plains relied on the buffalo for food, clothing, and other necessities, the animals' destruction made the Indians' lives much more difficult. (Later in his life, Will would push his friend President Theodore Roosevelt to establish national parks and pass laws to help preserve the buffalo and other wildlife.)

In the summer of 1868, Will returned to work with the U.S. Army and was soon named chief scout of the Fifth Cavalry under General Philip Sheridan. Will was very popular with the men of the Fifth, who considered him their good luck charm. Between 1868 and 1872, he took part in 14 battles against Native American warriors and, for his outstanding service, was awarded the Congressional Medal of Honor in 1872.

Sitting Bull

The man known as Sitting Bull was born around 1831 in what is now South Dakota. His tribal name was *Tatanka-Iyotanka*, which describes how a buffalo bull looks when it sits defiantly on its haunches. Sitting Bull became head chief of the Hunkpapa Lakota Sioux around 1868. In the mid-1870s, he risked war by refusing to lead his people onto a reservation so that white prospectors could freely dig for gold in the Black Hills area of South Dakota, which was sacred to his people. On June 25, 1876, Sitting Bull's warriors wiped out troops led by General George Custer at the Little Bighorn in Montana. He later surrendered and was imprisoned. In 1885, he was allowed to leave the reservation to join *Buffalo Bill's Wild West* for one season and became the show's biggest attraction. In 1890, Sitting Bull was killed by Indian police (Native Americans working for the Indian Bureau) who came to arrest him, fearing he might lead the Lakota in a new war.

By that time, the name "Buffalo Bill" Cody was already famous throughout the country. He was the hero of many dime novels— paperback thrillers costing 10 cents each—and was a stage star as well. The Buffalo Bill stories and plays, which mixed a little truth with a lot of fiction, helped bring the Wild West to life for Americans who dreamed of having more adventure in their own lives.

Just how had Will Cody become so famous? The answer was due in part to the efforts of a writer named Ned Buntline, who was looking to increase his own fame and fortune, and in part to Will's own flamboyant personality. When the two men got together in 1869, they helped set off a revolution in American entertainment history.

Buntline, who was traveling throughout the West looking for story ideas, had heard about the recent battle of Summit Springs in which Will had accompanied troops in an attack on a Cheyenne camp to rescue two white women being held captive. Most of the Cheyenne were killed, and one of the white women was saved. During the fighting, Will faced off against the Cheyenne chief Tall Bull, shot him, and captured his magnificent horse. Will rode the horse proudly back to the army fort. The fight added to Will's reputation and helped convince Buntline that Will Cody was the man to feature in his Western novels. The men talked briefly, and Will, of course, shared many stories of his life on the plains.

In December 1869, the first episode of a new novel entitled *Buffalo Bill, the King of the Border Men* appeared in a New York newspaper. The plot came mostly from Buntline's imagination, but it thrilled readers. Buntline's "Buffalo Bill" overcame deadly Indians and dastardly bandits, saved women in distress, was kind but firm, and spoke the way Easterners imagined Western scouts would talk. For example, early in the book, Bill exclaims, "You base cowards . . . I will kill every father's son of you before the beard grows on my face!" The book was so successful that Buntline and other authors began writing new ones. Over the next 20 years, more than 500 best-selling Buffalo Bill thrillers were published.

In 1872, Buntline wrote and produced a play called *The Scouts of the Plains.* It was a poorly connected mixture of scenes based on several different Buffalo Bill adventures. Buntline talked Will into playing himself on the stage. Will was worried about having stage fright, but he agreed to try after Buntline convinced him that "there is money to be made." The play opened in Chicago, Illinois. It received terrible reviews from critics, but audiences loved it. It was performed in theaters around the country for the next 10 years. Will acted in that play and in several spin-offs as well. He also took over the theater company from Buntline. He would spend each fall and winter as an actor and then return to the plains to work as an army scout during the spring and summer. Buffalo Bill the showman was born.

Not everything in Will's life was going perfectly, however. In 1870, Louisa and Will had a son, whom they named Kit Carson Cody, after the famous frontier scout. When Kit died from scarlet fever in April 1876, Will was heartbroken; however, he didn't have much time to grieve. The Sioux and Lakota were uprising in

THE BUFFALO BILL STORIES

A WEEKLY PUBLICATION

DEVOTED TO BORDER HISTORY

Issued Weekly. By Subscription $2.50 per year. Entered as Second Class Matter at New York Post Office by STREET & SMITH, 238 William St., N. Y.

No. 137.

Price, Five Cents.

BUFFALO BILL IN THE BLACK HILLS

or RED HAND, THE WHITE MYSTERY

Dime novels published by Ned Buntline were a hot commodity in the late 1800s but were considered taboo reading for children.

the Black Hills area of South Dakota, and Will rushed back to assume his scouting duties. On June 25, a band of warriors led by chiefs Sitting Bull and Crazy Horse encountered a division of the Seventh Cavalry under General George Armstrong Custer. All of the soldiers were killed in the battle.

A few weeks later, Will was leading a scouting party from the Fifth Cavalry when they spotted a band of Cheyenne warriors near War Bonnet Creek. Will was wearing an unusual outfit that day—a fringed black velvet suit that he often wore on the stage. Some historians believe Will wore the suit so he could show off his "fighting clothes" to audiences the following winter. Will noticed some Indians riding toward another group of soldiers nearby, and he raced into action. He shot and killed the Cheyenne leader, known as Yellow Hand, and then scalped him. Holding up the topknot, Will is supposed to have shouted, "The first scalp for Custer!" Will would play this scene over and over in his Wild West shows in later years and display Yellow Hand's feathered headdress and the scalp for audiences to admire. The story added to the growing legend of Buffalo Bill.

Meeting Ned Buntline

Meeting Ned Buntline in 1869 helped change Will Cody's life, but just how did the two men meet? According to one story, Buntline thought the hero of the battle of Summit Springs was another scout—Frank North. Buntline sought out North and asked if he would like to become the star of some Western thrillers that Buntline planned to write. North declined but pointed to Will Cody, who was sleeping under a wagon nearby, and jokingly said, "There's the man you're looking for." Buntline woke Will and explained his dime novel idea, and Will readily agreed. The story goes on to credit Buntline with creating the catchy name "Buffalo Bill" for his main character. But Will Cody was already widely known as Buffalo Bill since he won the buffalo killing contest in 1867. Also, North never mentioned meeting Buntline in his own writings about his army service. It is more likely that Buntline sought out Buffalo Bill directly and was impressed by his outgoing personality and the stories Cody told of his exploits.

General George Armstrong Custer and his cavalry are killed at the Battle of the Little Big Horn.

CHAPTER THREE

Bringing the West to Life

WILL CODY WAS NOW A HERO ON BOTH
THE WESTERN PLAINS
AND THE EASTERN STAGES, AND HE LOVED THE ATTENTION.

Will's long, flowing hair, upright stature, and fancy clothes helped him
STAND OUT WHEREVER HE WENT.

There was one drawback to his new life—being away from

home so much damaged his relationship with his wife

and three daughters—but Will was having too much fun

and making too much money to worry about that. Audi-

ences continued to pack theaters to see his acting company

perform, and Buffalo Bill novels were a big hit, keeping

his name before the public. All of this convinced Will to

give up scouting and focus on show business full-time.

For several years, Will had thought about creating a touring Wild West show. Then, in 1882, he saw an opportunity to put his ideas into action. The Cody family was then living near North Platte, Nebraska. It was already June, and Will realized that the town had no plans for a big Independence Day celebration. He approached the town leaders and proposed a show celebrating the "real West." It would be more than a rodeo and different from a circus, Will promised. He called it the *Old Glory Blowout*.

The show was a big success. On July 4, North Platte overflowed with spectators, who cheered for their country and for Buffalo Bill. "I tried out my idea on my neighbors, and they lived through it and liked it," Will said, "so I made up my mind right then I'd take the show east." Actually, he went only as far east as Omaha for the first performance of *The Wild West, Rocky Mountain, and Prairie Exhibition*, which opened on May 17, 1883. From there it moved on to other Midwestern towns.

Will's new show featured cowboys doing rope tricks, Pawnee Indians racing bareback ponies, "bandits" attacking a stagecoach, a dramatization of a Pony Express rider switching horses on the fly, a trick marksman, a small buffalo stampede, and more. The show lasted for hours, but audiences never were bored.

There were some problems, however. With so many actors, Will had trouble keeping everything moving smoothly. Some performers were off on their timing, and others were sometimes too drunk to perform. Will, too, was known to drink heavily after a show. There

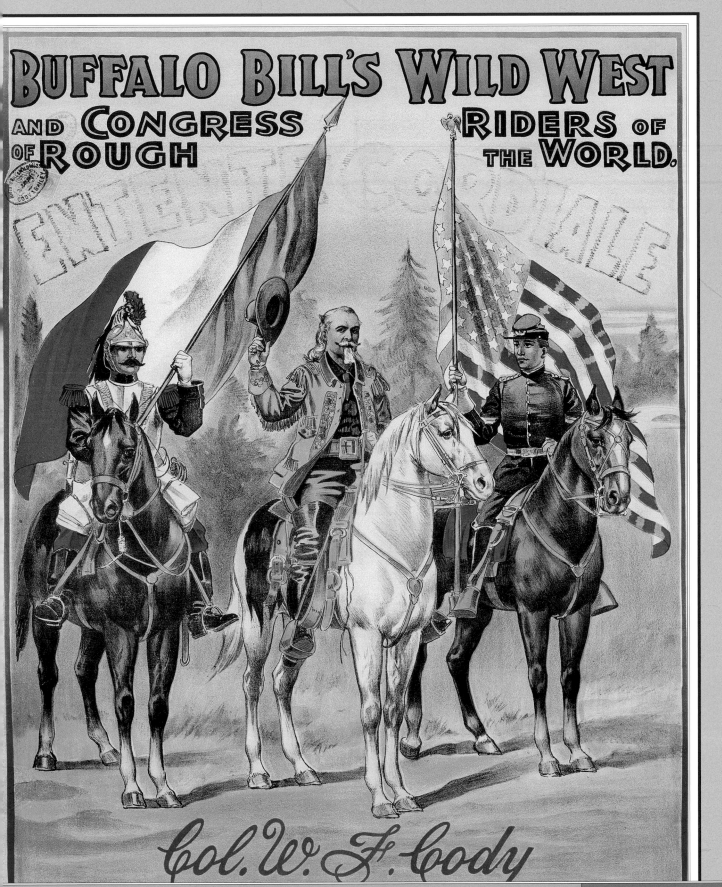

Buffalo Bill's Wild West *attracted and captivated vast audiences in both America and Europe at the turn of the 19th century.*

Annie Oakley

Phoebe Anne (Annie) Moses was born in 1860 in Darke County, Ohio. Annie's father died when she was only six, and she spent several years living in an orphanage and a foster home before her mother was financially able to take her back. She then taught herself to shoot her father's old rifle and helped support her family by hunting game for a Cincinnati hotel. When the hotel sponsored a shooting contest, Annie entered and won, defeating a champion marksman named Frank Butler. Annie and Frank later married and developed a circus act in which she was billed as "Annie Oakley." In 1885, Annie joined *Buffalo Bill's Wild West* and became one of its main attractions. During her act, she would use pinpoint accuracy to snuff out candles, knock a cigarette out of Frank's mouth, shoot apples off the head of her poodle, and fire backwards over her shoulder while looking in a mirror. When Sitting Bull joined the show, he called Annie "Little Sure Shot," and from then on, that was how she was introduced to audiences.

was also the problem of transporting all of the people, animals, and equipment when the show moved to new locations.

Thankfully, by the next season, most of the problems had been ironed out. Now, the three-hour extravaganza ran like clockwork, and the excitement never let up. Will even added a big finale, a reenactment of Custer's Last Stand in which some of the Sioux warriors who had fought at the Little Bighorn played parts. At the end, Will would ride onstage in his scouting outfit and shake his head sadly, while a banner appeared behind the actors proclaiming: "Too Late!"

Following a performance in New Orleans, Louisiana, late in the season, a tiny young woman sought out Will and asked to join the show. Standing barely five feet (1.5 m) tall, she looked like a teenager, even though she was 25. She said her name was Annie Oakley, and she was the best trick-shooter around. Will gave her an audition and was impressed. Annie joined the show the next season and stayed on until 1901, when an injury suffered during a train accident left her partially paralyzed.

The company opened its 1885 season under a new name: *Buffalo Bill's Wild West*. The word "show" was purposely omitted to emphasize how real everything would be. Will even convinced Sitting Bull to appear. The Lakota chief would ride a horse onstage and stand before the audience with a look of great dignity. Some people booed, but he showed no emotion. While it may seem today that Buffalo Bill was exploiting Sitting Bull by having him appear, the

Buffalo Bill (front, right) was dignified in his treatment of Indian performers such as Chief Sitting Bull (back, center) .

truth was that the chief badly needed his weekly $50 salary and the money he was earning from the hundreds of photographs he sold after performances. Sitting Bull also considered Will a friend who treated him and other Native Americans fairly.

Buffalo Bill's Wild West was a roaring success. Charging general admission prices of 50 cents for adults and 25 cents for children (more for reserved seats and boxes), the show took in more than $1 million in gate receipts in 1885, and Will shared profits of $100,000 with his partner, Nate Salsbury. ($100,000 in 1885 would be worth around $2 million today.) Will spent part of his money to fix up a new ranch near North Platte. When he wasn't traveling, Will lived there with Louisa and their daughters.

Buffalo Bill's Wild West thrilled and fascinated audiences for more than 25 years. Will once estimated that more than 50 million people had watched him perform. The show made an era of American history come to life for audiences in the United States and in Europe, too. Starting in 1887, the Wild West played to nearly 40,000 people a day in England and France for six seasons, before Will brought it home for the World's Columbian Exposition (also known as the World's Fair) in Chicago in 1893.

But Will still had one more way in mind to leave his mark on the West. Starting in 1896, he and a group of investors formed the Shoshone Land and Irrigation Company to develop desert areas in northwestern Wyoming, not far from Yellowstone Park. The group planned a model modern town, called Cody. Will poured much of his own money into Cody, Wyoming, and nearly went broke in the process. When Will had trouble in the early 1900s obtaining funds to establish hydroelectric power for the region, he convinced President Roosevelt to build a dam nearby using government money. Completed in 1910, the Shoshone Dam and Reservoir provided the region with the drinking water and power it needed. Will also persuaded Roosevelt to establish a national forest in the region.

In 1905, Will sued his wife for divorce after 39 years, claiming that she was always nagging him and never supported what he did. Louisa, in turn, claimed that Will was seldom home and was sometimes unfaithful to her. In the end, they decided to drop the divorce but lived apart the rest of Will's life.

Then, starting in 1907, the *Wild West* began losing popularity and money. In 1912, Will took out a loan from a dishonest banker to keep the show afloat. The next year, the banker called in the loan, and Will had to give up control of the show and sell off much of its equipment to pay his debts. Tired and discouraged, Will's health began to decline. On January 10, 1917, he died at his sister May's house in Denver, Colorado.

Meeting His Future Wife

Will and Louisa (Lulu) Cody had an unusual relationship. They had very different personalities and spent most of their married life apart. Many different stories were told about how they met in St. Louis in 1865. According to one story, Louisa was with some girlfriends when a group of drunken soldiers began bothering them. Will jumped in and ordered the soldiers to leave the girls alone. While an argument ensued, all of the girls ran home except Louisa, who was too frightened to move. Will walked her home, and they soon fell in love. Another story said that the couple met when Will rescued Louisa, who was riding on a horse that was out of control. Louisa described the real way they met in her memoir. Her cousin William became friends with Will in St. Louis and introduced the couple. At their first meeting, Will playfully tried to pull a chair out from under Louisa, and she slapped him. They later made up and became engaged.

CHAPTER FOUR

The Showman Lives On

BUFFALO BILL'S
DEATH WAS MOURNED BY EVERYONE,
from world leaders
TO LITTLE CHILDREN.

Even Native American tribes sent their condolences. One telegram from the chief of the Ogala Sioux in South Dakota read:

"The Ogalas found in Buffalo Bill a warm and lasting friend. … Our hearts are sad from the heavy burden of his passing, lightening only in the belief in our meeting before the presence of our Wakan Tanka [Grandfather Spirit] in the great hunting ground."

In 1912, an aging Buffalo Bill was saddened to see his show go by the wayside. He had been a showman for nearly 30 years.

Over the next few years, stories and interviews filled American newspapers, praising Buffalo Bill and adding to his fame. Then, something unexpected began to happen. Beginning in the late 1920s, some writers and historians started questioning how many of the Buffalo Bill legends were true and how many were fiction. The writers backed up their opinions with quotes from men who had known Will or worked with him. Still, it was hard to tell if the people who called Buffalo Bill a fake were telling the truth themselves or just motivated by jealousy.

One old-time cowboy, Teddy Blue Abbott, said, "Buffalo Bill was a good fellow, and while he was no great shakes as a scout as he made the eastern people believe, still we all liked him and we had to hand it to him because he was the only one that had brains enough to make that Wild West stuff pay money."

But Abbott's comments don't ring true. The record on Will Cody's success as a scout and his bravery is very strong. He was continually rehired by the cavalry and even kept on the payroll during the winters when he wasn't scouting. He earned promotions and raises, and he was awarded the Congressional Medal of Honor for his service. It is possible that Will sometimes took more credit than he deserved for his actions in battle—or was given more credit by writers—but he never backed down from an assignment or held back in a battle. In fact, in incidents such as the fight with Yellow Hand at War Bonnet Creek, Will was the first man on the scene.

Ned Buntline

No one did more to make Buffalo Bill a national folk hero than writer Ned Buntline. Buntline, whose real name was E. Z. C. Judson, was born in 1823 and served in the U.S. Navy in the 1840s. One of his shipboard jobs was to tighten the buntlines fastened to the bottom of sails. After leaving the navy, he became a writer under the pen name "Ned Buntline," specializing in sensational stories. He later served in the Union Army in the Civil War but was dishonorably discharged for drunkenness. Buntline returned to writing and looked to the Wild West for new stories to excite his readers. He met Buffalo Bill Cody in 1869 and made him the hero of his novel *Buffalo Bill, the King of the Border Men.* Buntline later wrote a play based on the exploits of Buffalo Bill and convinced Cody to play himself onstage. Buntline also wrote novels about other Western heroes such as Wyatt Earp and Wild Bill Hickok.

Another criticism leveled at Buffalo Bill involved how he portrayed Native Americans in his shows or treated his Native American actors. For example, some writers wondered whether reenacting Custer's Last Stand might have flamed resentment against Native Americans or whether bringing Sitting Bull out before audiences belittled the proud chief. Buffalo Bill would have objected strongly to both criticisms. He felt that by having Indians in his show, audiences would become more aware of their hard life on the plains and more respectful of their culture. He never allowed a white actor to portray a Native American in his shows. He wanted to make sure audiences believed that what they were seeing was real. And he always made sure that the Native Americans in his shows were treated fairly.

Sitting Bull himself agreed to be in the *Wild West*, not only for financial reasons but also because he had respect for Buffalo Bill. The Lakota chief prized a white Stetson hat that Will had given him. Once when a relative touched the hat, Sitting Bull snatched it away, saying, "My friend Pahaska ('Long-Hair') gave me this hat. I value it highly, for the hand that placed it on my head had friendly feeling for me."

Sitting Bull even requested that Buffalo Bill serve as a middleman in talks with white leaders in 1890, before the chief was arrested and murdered. The Indian agent who had ordered Sitting Bull's arrest would not permit Buffalo Bill to get involved. It always saddened Will that he was unable to help prevent the chief's death.

While the criticisms leveled against him might have saddened Buffalo Bill, he would be proud of his legacy. In many ways, the modern rodeo, with its trick riding and roping events, grew out of the *Wild West*. So did reenacted cattle drives and dude ranches. Even expressions such as "circling the wagons" and "riding off into the sunset" became popular after they were used by actors in Buffalo Bill's shows.

Buffalo Bill's memory is kept alive in a direct way each year with different shows and festivals. For example, the town of Sheridan, Wyoming, sponsors "Buffalo Bill Days" each June. Visitors can observe a grand ball with attendees in 1890s Western dress and watch an exciting Wild West show. The festival posts a Web site at http://www.buffalobilldays.org that includes photos of events and interesting facts about Buffalo Bill. The city of North Platte, Nebraska, where Buffalo Bill first tried out his Wild West show idea, holds a Buffalo Bill Rodeo each year as part of the "Nebraskaland Days" celebration of the state's history. And a modern-day *Buffalo Bill's Wild West* is even part of EuroDisney in France.

Will Cody's legacy goes beyond show business, too. For example, the city of Cody, Wyoming, which he helped develop, is now a thriving community with nearly 9,000 residents. More than one million tourists visit Cody each year, and many stay or dine at the Hotel Irma, named for Will's youngest daughter. The nearby dam for which Will helped raise funds still provides water and power for the entire Big Horn Valley. Its name was changed from Shoshone Dam to Buffalo Bill Dam in 1946.

This bronze sculpture of Buffalo Bill on horseback was created in 1924 and continues to overlook the city of Cody, Wyoming.

Buffalo Bill also influenced the arts. He commissioned paintings of Western scenes by artists such as Frederic Remington and Charles Shreyvogel. The paintings are still displayed in museums today and help keep the Old West alive. Buffalo Bill is also one of the "fathers" of the Western film. He acted in the first western ever produced, *Congress of Rough Riders*, made by the Edison Company in 1893. Then, in 1913, he began making his own movie about the history of the Wild West and the Indian wars. Not much of that film survives today, unfortunately. He was also brought to life in several popular westerns of the 1930s and 1940s, such as *Buffalo Bill* (1944) and *My Darling Clementine* (1946), both of which are sometimes shown on late-night television.

William Frederick Cody was more directly involved in the key moments in the history of the American West than almost any other man, but his life story is much more thrilling than a history book. An adventurer, a soldier, and a showman—Buffalo Bill lived in the Wild West, and then he recreated the excitement of that place and time for millions of others who could experience it only secondhand. Perhaps no one enjoyed being a legend more than Buffalo Bill or more successfully blended fact with fiction. According to one final legend, Will's last words were, "Let my show go on." His wish has come true.

Burying Buffalo Bill

Buffalo Bill is buried on Lookout Mountain near Denver, Colorado, and scores of tourists regularly visit his gravesite there. But, according to some historians, Lookout Mountain isn't where he wanted to be laid to rest. Will had another place in mind—Cedar Mountain, overlooking Cody, Wyoming. He wrote his sister Julia in 1902: "I have got a mountain picked out big enough for all of us to be buried on." So why is his grave in Colorado instead? According to Louisa Cody's autobiography, Will changed his mind the night before he died. He told her he wanted to be buried on Lookout Mountain, where he could look down on four states. Some people have speculated that Louisa received a large bribe from the city of Denver to help pay for the funeral expenses, but no one is certain. In any case, Will's funeral was described as "the most impressive and most largely attended ever seen in the West"—a fitting ending for a great showman.

Further Information

BOOKS

Carter, Robert A. *Buffalo Bill: The Man Behind the Legend*.
New York: John Wiley & Sons, 2000.

Russell, Don. *The Lives and Legends of Buffalo Bill*. Norman, Okla.:
University of Oklahoma Press, 1975.

Wilson, R. L., and Greg Martin. *Buffalo Bill's Wild West: An American Legend*.
New York: Random House, 1998.

FILMS

Buffalo Bill: Showman of the West. 1996. 50 min. A&E Home Video.

Buffalo Bill's Wild West Show. 1987. 45 min. The Old Army Press.

The Plainsman. 1987 (videocassette release of 1937 motion picture).
113 min. MCA Home Video.

WEB SITES

Buffalo Bill Grave and Museum
http://www.buffalobill.org

Buffalo Bill Historical Center
http://www.bbhc.org

William F. Cody (Buffalo Bill)
http://www.americanwest.com/pages/buffbill.htm

Index